THROUGH HER EYES: FINDING JOY BEYOND GLUTEN

"A FAMILY'S JOURNEY THROUGH LOVE, RESILIENCE, AWARENESS, AND GLUTEN-FREE LIVING"

AF428924

POOJA PAL

VIKAS SINGH

To my beloved daughter, Manviya Singh,

This book is dedicated to you, my courageous and resilient princess. From the day you were born, you have been a source of immense joy and inspiration for our family. Your strength in facing the challenges of celiac disease with grace and determination is a testament to your incredible spirit.

May this book serve as a reminder of your unwavering strength and the love that surrounds you. Through every trial and triumph, you have taught us the true meaning of hope and resilience. We are so proud of you, and we will always stand by your side as you navigate this journey.

With all my love,

Pooja Pal

Contents

Foreword

Once upon a time in a bustling household filled with laughter and love, a small mystery began to unfold. It started with the youngest member of the Singh family, a vibrant and joyful little girl named Manviya. From the moment she was born, Manviya was a beacon of light, her laughter echoing through the hallways and her playful spirit bringing smiles to everyone she met.

As Manviya grew, her parents, Mr. and Mrs. Singh, noticed subtle changes. What began as occasional tummy aches turned into persistent discomfort, and Manviya's bright eyes often seemed clouded with fatigue. Despite their best efforts to find answers, the mystery deepened. Endless doctor visits and tests left the family anxious and worried, but they never lost hope.

Then, one fateful day, a compassionate doctor, Dr. D.V. Umesh Reddy, suggested a possibility that had been overlooked. Tests were run, and the results confirmed it: Manviya had celiac disease. The revelation was both a shock and a relief. At last, they had an answer, but it came with a new challenge—navigating a gluten-free world.

Manviya, with her innate courage and determination, became a symbol of hope for the entire family. Her journey inspired them to educate others, advocate for awareness, and create a future filled with joy and possibility. This book, "Through Her Eyes: Finding Joy Beyond Gluten," is a testament to their journey.

It is a story of love, resilience, and the unyielding spirit of a family determined to thrive despite the obstacles. Through these pages, Whether you are a parent of a child with any gluten medical condition, a caregiver, or someone navigating this condition yourself, this book is for you. It is a reminder that you are not alone and that together, we can find joy and strength beyond gluten.

With heartfelt gratitude to Dr. D.V. Umesh Reddy and the Post Graduate Institute of Child Health, Noida, for their unwavering support.

Welcome to our story.

Pooja Pal

Preface

In the bustling city of Dehradun, within a cozy and loving household, lived the Singh family. Their home was filled with laughter, shared meals, and the joyous giggles of their little girl, Manviya. From the moment she was born, she brought light and happiness wherever she went, cherished deeply by her parents and younger brother, Parikshit.

As the years passed, their vibrant and energetic daughter began experiencing frequent stomach aches and fatigue. Numerous doctor visits and countless tests left the family searching for answers. Finally, a diagnosis of celiac disease provided clarity but also marked the beginning of a new journey.

Transitioning to a gluten-free lifestyle was both challenging and transformative. The family's kitchen became a hub of experimentation, filled with successes, setbacks, and plenty of laughter. Through it all, they discovered that joy wasn't confined to the foods they once loved but could be found in the bonds they strengthened and the resilience they built together.

This book, "Through Her Eyes: Finding Joy Beyond Gluten," is a heartfelt account of their journey. It is a story of resilience, adaptation, and an unyielding bond. Through Manviya's eyes, we witness the struggles and triumphs, tears and laughter, and the unwavering hope that carried them forward.

To every parent navigating new paths and to every child showing incredible strength—this story is for you. It's about embracing life's challenges with love, courage, and the belief that happiness lies in the moments and memories we create.

To my brave and joyful little star, Manviya, thank you for inspiring me every day. This is our story, and I couldn't be prouder to share it with the world.

With love and gratitude,
Pooja Pal

Acknowledgements

As I sit down to write these acknowledgements, I am filled with immense gratitude for the many individuals who have played a crucial role in our journey and the creation of this book, "Through Her Eyes: Finding Joy Beyond Gluten."

This journey began with my beloved daughter Manviya, your bravery in the face of challenges has shown me the true meaning of strength. Thank you for being the heart and soul of this story.

To my husband, Vikas Singh, thank you for your unwavering support and for being my rock through every twist and turn. Your love and encouragement have made it possible for us to navigate this journey together, and I am forever grateful for your partnership.

My deepest thanks go to Dr. D.V. Umesh Reddy, whose expertise and compassion led us to the diagnosis that changed our lives. Your guidance has been invaluable, and we owe so much of our understanding and management of celiac disease to your support.

To the wonderful team at the Post Graduate Institute of Child Health, Noida, thank you for your dedication to our family's well-being. Your care and professionalism have made a significant impact on our lives, and we are incredibly grateful for your efforts.

A special mention goes to my extended family specially aunt Neeta and friends, who have walked this path with us. Your love, patience, and understanding have provided us with the strength to face each day with hope and determination. Thank you for being our pillars of support.

To the celiac community, both near and far, your shared experiences and advice have been a lifeline for us. The sense of belonging and solidarity within this community has made our journey more manageable, and we are thankful for the connections we have made along the way.

Finally, to my readers, thank you for taking the time to join us on this journey. Your interest and support mean the world to us, and we hope that our story brings you hope, guidance, and a sense of community.

This book is a testament to the power of love, resilience, and the unbreakable bonds of family. It is a reminder that even in the face of adversity, there is always a path to joy and healing. Thank you to everyone who has been a part of this journey—we could not have done it without you.

With heartfelt gratitude,

Pooja Pal

Prologue

In a warm and bustling home nestled in the heart of Dehradun, the Singh family's life was a tapestry of love, laughter, and cherished moments. Each day began with the familiar sounds of morning routines—the sizzle of breakfast on the stove, the soft hum of conversations, and the joyous giggles of their beloved daughter, Manviya. She was the heart of their home, her presence filling every corner with light and warmth.

As the years passed, subtle changes began to cast shadows over their happiness. Manviya, their vibrant and energetic princess, started to experience frequent tummy aches, fatigue, and mysterious symptoms that left them puzzled and concerned. The once joyful household was now tinged with worry and uncertainty, as countless doctor visits and tests yielded no answers.

It was during one of these desperate searches for clarity that they met Dr. D.V. Umesh Reddy, a compassionate medical practitioner who would change their lives forever. Through a series of tests and observations, Dr. Reddy diagnosed Manviya with celiac disease. The news was a mix of relief and trepidation—finally, they had an answer, but it also meant embarking on a challenging new journey.

Armed with determination and love, the Singh family set out to navigate the complexities of a gluten-free lifestyle. They transformed their kitchen, learned to read food labels meticulously, and adapted their daily routines to ensure Manviya's health and happiness. Along the way, they discovered a strength within themselves that they never knew existed.

"Through Her Eyes: Finding Joy Beyond Gluten" is the story of their journey. It chronicles the highs and lows, the tears and triumphs, and the unwavering hope that defined their path. It is a tale of resilience, adaptation, and the unbreakable bond of family.

As you turn these pages, you will walk alongside the Singh family, sharing in their struggles and celebrating their victories. You will see the world through Manviya's eyes, a world where joy and love can be found even in the face of adversity. This is their story, and it is one of hope, courage, and the enduring power of family.

Welcome to the journey.

Pooja Pal

CHAPTER ONE

INTRODUCTION OF FAMILY MEMBERS

"Through Her Eyes: Finding Joy Beyond Gluten" is an inspiring tale of love, resilience, and family bonds. It follows Mr. and Mrs. Singh's journey as they navigate parenthood and cherish their children, Manviya and Parikshit. Mr. Singh balances his humanitarian work with his heartfelt role as a father, while Mrs. Singh learns to embrace motherhood alongside her career aspirations. Manviya, the family's cherished princess, showcases strength and compassion, nurturing her mischievous brother Parikshit, whose playful chaos adds joy to their lives. This story is a heartwarming exploration of life's unexpected turns and the unbreakable bonds that define a family.

Mr. Singh

a dedicated father, and a devoted professional working with the United Nations, had always cherished the idea of having a family of his own. His life, focused on global missions and humanitarian work, took a personal turn when he learned that he is about to become a father. The anticipation of meeting his little one is something he had never quite prepared for.

After what felt like an eternity of waiting, the day finally arrived when Mr. Singh's leave from work is granted, and he could meet his precious daughter, Manviya. His heart raced as he made his way back home, eager to see the little girl he had only known through the voice of his wife's soft whispers on the phone.

When Mr. Singh first laid eyes on his baby girl, holding her in his arms for the very first time, he is overcome with emotion. His heart swelled with love, and his eyes filled with tears. Time seemed to stop in that fleeting moment as he held the tiny bundle in his arms, marvelling at her delicate features and the warmth of her tiny body. He had imagined this moment countless times, but nothing could compare to the overwhelming feeling of finally being a father.

With his fingers gently brushing through her soft hair, Mr. Singh whispered blessings to his daughter, his voice trembling with emotion. As he held her close, he felt an overwhelming connection, a bond that words could not express. She is his princess, his miracle, a gift from God—his prayers had been answered.

But in that sacred moment of connection, Mr. Singh froze for a brief second, taking in every detail of his daughter's face. He memorized the shape of her small nose, the curve of her lips, and the sparkle of her tiny eyes as they fluttered open. It is as if he were trying to imprint this memory into his soul, knowing that this precious little girl would change his life forever. He couldn't help but marvel at how much she resembled the image he had held in his heart all along. She is everything he had hoped for and more.

In the quiet of the room, as Mr. Singh held Manviya in his arms, he felt as if the world outside had paused. In that moment, nothing else mattered—his work, the challenges he faced in his career, the missions he had undertaken. All that mattered is his daughter, the beautiful gift that had come into his life. And with her, a new journey began, one that would be filled with love, laughter, and the challenges of being a father, raising a little girl who would soon show him the strength and courage of her spirit.

Mrs. Singh

In 2014, a woman married the love of her life, Mr. Singh, full of dreams and aspirations for a future together. They had just returned from their honeymoon, a time of pure bliss, when Mr. Singh, with a heart full of determination and love, left home once again for his professional commitments. As he walked away, he left her with eyes that were brimming with emotion, a mixture of love and longing.

Despite the sadness of his departure, the woman remained focused on her own dreams. She had always dreamed of becoming a bank officer, a goal she had worked tirelessly toward. Having already cleared the preliminary exams, she eagerly enrolled in a preparatory class to ensure her path to success is clear. She is filled with hope and determination, looking ahead to a bright career in banking.

However, just a month into her preparations, something unexpected happened. She realized that she hadn't had her period, something that had never occurred before. Concerned, she consulted with a doctor, only to be met with a shocking revelation. She is pregnant.

The news hit her like a wave, leaving her stunned and unsure. How could this be happening now? She had worked so hard to build her future, and a career in banking is within her reach. She had always envisioned a life of independence, one where her career would define her, and now this unexpected turn seemed to threaten everything she had planned.

The initial shock gave way to confusion and fear. She isn't sure how to reconcile her dreams with this sudden reality. But as days passed, something inside her began to change. She started to understand the deeper meaning of the news. The thought of becoming a mother began to take root in her heart. She realized that being a mother is not a detour from her dreams, but a new journey that could coexist with her aspirations.

With time, she embraced her pregnancy, understanding that this is a new chapter, one that would bring a different kind of fulfilment and joy. She is no longer just a woman with a career dream; she is about to become a mother, a role that would shape her in ways she never imagined. The woman learned to balance her dreams of a bright career with the love and responsibility of motherhood, and in doing so, she discovered a new strength within herself. The road ahead would be different, but it would be her own, and she would navigate it with courage and grace.

The annoying sweet sibling

At the age of four, Manviya's life took a beautiful turn when her prayers, whispered with the innocence of a child, were answered. She is blessed with a baby brother, Parikshit—a precious gift from God. His arrival is nothing short of a miracle. Parikshit's journey into the world is not an easy one; he faced struggles that tested his tiny body, but with resilience and the unwavering love of his family, he won the fight to stay.

From the very beginning, Parikshit made his presence known in the family. Like any younger sibling, he had a knack for seeking attention, and he did so in ways that both frustrated and amused Manviya. Whether it is biting her, pulling her hair, destroying her carefully crafted artwork, or hiding behind furniture after his mischief, Parikshit is a master of playful chaos. His antics often left Manviya exasperated, but they also brought laughter and joy to the household.

Despite his mischievous ways, the bond between Manviya and Parikshit grew deeper with each passing day. Beneath the teasing and squabbles is a love that is pure and unwavering. When Parikshit fell ill, this is Manviya who stepped into the role of a protective elder sister. She would diligently give him his medication, carefully measure his temperature, and even place cold sponges on his forehead to bring him comfort. Her nurturing spirit shone brightly, and in those moments, the sibling rivalry is replaced by a tenderness that melted the hearts of their parents.

Parikshit, for all his attention-seeking ways, adored his sister just as much. He looked up to her, even when he is pulling her hair or toppling her towers of blocks. And Manviya, despite her occasional complaints, couldn't imagine her world without him. He is her little brother, her partner in adventure, and her forever friend.

Their bond, like any sibling relationship, is filled with ups and downs, laughter and tears, but at its core is an unbreakable love. Together, they created a world of their own, one filled with mischief, care, and countless memories. Parikshit may have been the master of playful chaos, but he is also the heart of Manviya's childhood, a reminder of the power of family and the beauty of growing up together.

The Princess Manviya

Manviya is not just a child; she is the cherished dream of Mr. and Mrs. Singh—a vision of love and hope they had held close long before she came into their lives. She is their princess, their joy, and the thread that wove their family closer together.

By the age of 8, Manviya's life is a delightful whirlwind. She had a younger brother, Parikshit, who, like most little brothers, is a bundle of mischief and energy. Whether it is pulling her hair, hiding her favourite belongings, or simply demanding her attention at every turn, Parikshit knew exactly how to test his sister's patience. Yet, despite the endless teasing, Manviya adored him and cared for him deeply. She would measure his temperature when he is sick, give him his medicine, and comfort him with a tenderness that only an elder sister could provide.

Adding to the lively mix were her cousins, Rudhvik and Arnika. Their presence brought even more joy and challenges into Manviya's life. As the eldest among them all, she took her role seriously, often stepping in to mediate their squabbles or to shield them from trouble. Though their antics could be exasperating, Manviya never let her frustration overshadow her love for them. She understood that being an elder sister is not just about correcting them but also about teaching them the value of family and care.

Manviya's journey as a sister, cousin, and the heart of her family is a testament to her strength and compassion. She may have been only 8, but her ability to love, nurture, and lead is beyond her years. To her family, she is more than just their princess—she is their glue, holding them together with her unwavering love and endless patience.

CHAPTER TWO

The Beginning of the Mystery

? The Joyful Routine: The Joyful Routine

Life in our little household is like a symphony, each moment resonating with laughter, love, and the lively chaos of raising our spirited daughter, Manviya. She is the heartbeat of our family, our little princess who brought colour and warmth to every corner of our lives.

From the moment she opened her eyes each morning, the world seemed brighter. Her laughter is infectious, a melody that echoed through the house and drew everyone into her orbit. Manviya has a gift for turning the simplest moments into magical ones. Whether it is dancing to her favourite tunes in the living room or chasing butterflies in the garden, her vibrant energy made the ordinary extraordinary.

She adored playing outdoors, her tiny feet pattering against the earth as she explored every nook and cranny. Her boundless curiosity led her to collect treasures—pebbles, leaves, and the occasional flower she would gift with a proud grin. These small, heartfelt gestures reminded us of the beauty in life's little things.

When she isn't outside, she could be found in the kitchen, her apron far too big for her small frame, yet she wore it with pride. She loved helping, her tiny hands eager to stir, pour, or taste. The clatter of pots and pans mixed with her giggles created a symphony of its own. Her favourite part? Rolling out dough, which often ended up more on her face than on the counter. But she didn't care, and neither did we.

In those moments, our kitchen became more than a place to cook; it became a space of togetherness and shared laughter. Her enthusiasm for being involved, no matter how small the task, brought us closer.

Manviya's presence is like sunshine. She has this incredible ability to make everyone feel special. Whether it is her grandparents, cousins, or the neighbourhood kids, her joy is contagious. She became the glue that bound us all together, her laughter weaving a tapestry of happiness in our lives.

Our days were filled with the rhythm of her energy and the love she so effortlessly shared. It is a simple, beautiful life—a routine that felt like a blessing. Little did we know, these joyful moments were about to face a shadow, one that would test our strength and unity as a family. But for now, we revelled in the joy she brought, cherishing every giggle, every hug, and every messy, dough-filled moment in the kitchen.

Manviya isn't just our daughter; she is the light that illuminated our path, reminding us of the beauty of living in the present, every day. Her love for life is infectious, and her warmth turned our house into a home filled with memories we would carry forever.

? The First Signs: The Subtle Signs

Our lively, ever-smiling daughter, Manviya, is the picture of health and happiness. She is full of energy, her days bursting with laughter, outdoor adventures, and playful banter. But slowly, almost imperceptibly at first, things began to change.

It started with the occasional stomach-ache—nothing too alarming, we thought. She must have eaten something that didn't agree with her, we told ourselves. Then came the irritability. Our usually cheerful little girl would sometimes snap or retreat into silence, moments that felt so out of character for her.

Over time, other troubling signs emerged. She began experiencing bouts of vomiting and constipation that left her visibly uncomfortable. Her once boundless energy seemed to wane, replaced by a weariness that no amount of rest could fix. We chalked it up to the usual suspects—maybe it is the pressure of school, a passing bug, or just one of those inexplicable phases that children go through.

Kids get sick, we reassured ourselves, brushing aside our growing concerns. We tried home remedies and adjusted her diet, hoping the symptoms would disappear as quickly as they had come. But they didn't.

Instead, they became more frequent, more pronounced, and impossible to ignore.

It is as though a shadow had begun creeping into her bright world, dimming the spark that defined her. The girl who once ran through the garden with uncontainable glee now often sat quietly, her small hands clutching her stomach, her smile fading into a look of discomfort.

Still, we hesitated. Is it really something to worry about? Or were we overreacting, like parents sometimes do? Looking back now, it's clear that we were trying to convince ourselves everything is fine because the alternative is too frightening to consider.

Little did we know that these subtle, seemingly unrelated symptoms were the first whispers of a mystery that would change our lives forever. They were the gentle knock of a challenge we couldn't yet see, a test of resilience and love that is waiting just around the corner.

? Worry Deepens: The Shadow Grows

Manviya's laughter, once the soundtrack of our home, began to fade. The occasional complaints of stomach aches became more frequent, her irritability no longer just a fleeting mood but an unsettling regularity. Episodes of vomiting and constipation disrupted her routines, and fatigue seemed to drape itself over her like an unwelcome guest.

What started as subtle changes now felt like an undeniable shift. The carefree little girl who loved chasing butterflies and whipping up cookies in the kitchen seemed burdened by something none of us could see.

Her bright smile, the one that could light up even the gloomiest days, began to falter. We noticed how her energy waned—how she would sometimes sit quietly, withdrawing from the activities she once loved. Her laughter, though still present, felt tinged with exhaustion.

At first, we tried to maintain a sense of normalcy, chalking it up to common childhood ailments. Maybe it's just a growth spurt, we told ourselves. Kids go through phases, don't they? But deep down, worry began to take root.

Her symptoms grew more severe, no longer content with fleeting appearances. They disrupted our daily lives, turning carefree afternoons into hurried doctor visits and sleepless nights. The concern that lingered at the edges of our thoughts transformed into full-blown worry as we scrambled for answers.

There were days when we felt helpless, watching her fight battles we couldn't understand. The playful sparkle in her eyes is now shadowed by discomfort and fatigue. Every giggle seemed hard-won; every moment of joy interrupted by the unrelenting grip of her symptoms.

We longed for the days when our biggest concern is which bedtime story to read. Now, our lives revolved around seeking explanations, navigating a maze of uncertainties, and hoping for a glimmer of understanding.

The shadow on her bright smile is impossible to ignore, and with every passing day, it loomed larger. We knew we couldn't wait any longer to confront it head-on. Something is wrong, and we had to find out what it is. Our little princess needed us to fight for her, even if we didn't yet know the battle we were facing.

? The Endless Search for Answers:

The journey to uncover the mystery behind Manviya's symptoms is anything but straightforward. Each symptom felt like a puzzle piece we couldn't place, and every visit to the doctor seemed to bring more questions than answers.

We shuffled through clinics and hospitals, our hopes pinned on each new consultation. Every doctor offered a possibility—an allergy, a virus, a digestive issue—but none of their diagnoses fully explained the relentless stomach aches, the irritability, or the constant fatigue that had taken hold of our little girl.

Countless tests became a part of our routine. Blood work, scans, and dietary evaluations filled our days, each one a step toward clarity—or so we hoped. But every result brought us back to the same frustrating conclusion: inconclusive.

The frustration began to mount. Each new appointment felt like a flicker of hope, only to be extinguished by another round of uncertainty. Watching Manviya endure these tests is heartbreaking. Her bravery shone through, but the process took its toll, leaving her weary and us emotionally drained.

Our home, once filled with laughter and playful chaos, is now a space of quiet concern and unanswered questions. We searched for patterns, reviewed her routines, and adjusted her diet, but nothing seemed to make a difference. It felt as though we were trapped in a never-ending loop, chasing a solution that remained just out of reach.

With every passing day, our frustration deepened. How could something so persistent remain so elusive? We trusted the process, yet it felt like we were running in circles, the weight of our confusion pressing down on us.

Despite it all, we refused to give up. Our determination to find answers for our princess kept us going. We knew that somewhere, there had to be a solution—a way to bring back her bright smile and free her from the shadow of these unexplained symptoms.

The search is exhausting, but it also brought us closer as a family. Together, we faced the frustration, shared the tears, and held onto hope. Little did we know, the answer is just around the corner, waiting to change our lives forever.

? A Pivotal Suggestion: A Glimmer of Hope

After months of unanswered questions and countless doctor visits, we found ourselves sitting in yet another consultation room, clinging to the hope that this time, there would be clarity. The specialist, an experienced and empathetic doctor, listened intently as we recounted Manviya's symptoms and the frustrating journey we'd been through.

After a moment of reflection, the specialist suggested something we had never considered—celiac disease. The words hung in the air, unfamiliar and mysterious. We exchanged puzzled glances. What is celiac disease? Could it be the answer we had been searching for?

The suggestion sparked a mix of emotions within us. On one hand, there is hope—perhaps this is the key to understanding what had been troubling our little girl. On the other hand, there is apprehension. What if this is just another false lead? What did a diagnosis of celiac disease even mean for her future?

The specialist patiently explained the condition, outlining how gluten—a common protein found in wheat, barley, and rye—could trigger severe reactions in those with celiac disease. It is a daunting thought. Gluten is everywhere, woven into the very fabric of our daily meals.

Despite our reservations, the doctor's calm and confident demeanour reassured us. This isn't just another guess; this is a direction, a potential breakthrough. The suggested test felt like a crossroads, a chance to finally uncover the truth after so much uncertainty.

As we left the clinic, we carried with us a strange combination of relief and nervous anticipation. The term celiac disease echoed in our minds, opening a door to new possibilities but also to unknown challenges.

Though apprehensive, we clung to the hope that this test might bring the clarity we desperately needed. Little did we know, this single suggestion would forever change the course of our lives, marking the beginning of a journey into understanding, adaptation, and resilience.

? The Life-Changing Diagnosis: The Moment of Truth

The day the test results arrived is etched in our memories—a day of revelation that changed everything. We sat in the doctor's clinic, holding our breath as the specialist reviewed the papers in front of him. His calm but serious expression spoke volumes.

It's confirmed, he said gently, looking up at us. Manviya has celiac disease.

The words landed like a jolt. In that instant, the months of confusion, endless questions, and sleepless nights condensed into a single, defining answer. The mystery that had overshadowed our lives finally had a name.

We met relief first, a wave of gratitude that we finally had clarity. No more guessing, no more futile tests—this is the answer we had been searching for. For the first time in what felt like forever, we understood what is happening to our little girl.

But relief is quickly followed by the weight of reality. The doctor began explaining what this diagnosis meant—a strict, lifelong gluten-free diet. No wheat, no barley, no rye. Foods we had taken for granted were now off-limits. The feeling of blackness surrounded us.

We looked at each other, absorbing the magnitude of the changes ahead. Meals would no longer be simple. Every ingredient, every meal, every outing would need scrutiny. It isn't just about food; it is about reshaping the very fabric of our daily lives.

And yet, as we glanced at Manviya, we saw her bright, curious eyes looking back at us, unaware of the gravity of the moment. Her innocence and resilience gave us strength. If she could adapt to this new reality, so could we.

As we left the doctor's clinic that day, our hearts were a mix of emotions—relief, determination, and a hint of fear. But above all, there is love. Love for our daughter, who would face this challenge with us. Love for each other, as we vowed to navigate this journey together.

This is our turning point—a moment that marked the end of uncertainty and the beginning of a new chapter. It is the start of a journey we never anticipated, but one we were ready to embrace, hand in hand with our little princess.

? New Beginnings: A New Chapter

Leaving the clinic, we stepped into a world that felt both unfamiliar and daunting. The diagnosis of celiac disease isn't just a label—it is an invitation into an entirely new way of life. Suddenly, we were faced with a challenge that required us to unlearn so much of what we knew and embrace a different reality.

The first step is education. We had dived into articles, books, and online resources, trying to grasp what celiac disease truly meant. The science behind it—the body's inability to tolerate gluten, the autoimmune response that damaged the small intestine—felt a curse at first. But as parents, we have no option but to understand every detail.

We pored over lists of gluten-containing foods, shocked at how many everyday items were now off-limits. Bread, pasta, cookies, and even seemingly harmless sauces and seasonings were suddenly scrutinized. Trips to the grocery store turned into long, meticulous hunts for gluten-free labels. Reading ingredient lists became second nature, and our kitchen started transforming into a gluten-free haven.

The learning curve isn't limited to food. We began to understand how cross-contamination could pose a risk—crumbs on a shared cutting board or a toaster used for regular bread could cause harm. It is daunting, but we knew that every precaution is an act of love for Manviya.

Through this process, adaptation became our mantra. We experimented with recipes, turning our kitchen into a place of discovery rather than restriction. Meals became a creative adventure, filled with new ingredients and flavours we had never considered before. Slowly but surely, the fear of the unknown gave way to confidence.

It isn't easy, though. There were moments of frustration, times when we mourned the simplicity of our old life. Watching Manviya long for a slice of cake at a party or hearing her ask why she couldn't eat what her friends were eating tugged at our hearts. But these moments also became opportunities to teach her about strength and resilience.

As a family, we grew closer. We were no longer just parents to a child with celiac disease—we were her advocates, her protectors, and her biggest cheerleaders. We navigated this journey as a team, learning to see the beauty in our shared struggles and triumphs.

Resilience became the cornerstone of our lives. Every challenge we faced—be it mastering gluten-free cooking, managing social situations, or helping Manviya understand her condition—strengthened our resolve. We were determined to ensure that her diagnosis would never dim her vibrant spirit or limit her potential.

This is the beginning of a journey that would shape us in ways we never imagined. It is a journey of adaptation, understanding, and unshakeable love—a journey that would remind us, time and again, of the strength we held as a family.

CHAPTER THREE

THE DIAGNOSIS

The diagnosis

The day the diagnosis came was both a relief and a shock. We had an answer at last, but it brought with it a new reality we hadn't prepared for. When the test results confirmed that Manviya had celiac disease, our emotions swirled. There was the relief of finally understanding the source of her struggles—the endless stomach aches, irritability, and fatigue—but it was quickly overtaken by the fear of what this meant for her future. Celiac disease wasn't just a dietary restriction; it was a life-altering condition

? THE Confirmation:

The day we received the test results will always remain etched in our minds as a day of both answers and a new beginning. The doctor's words, "Manviya has celiac disease," hit us like a sudden shockwave. The weight of those words lingered in the air, filling the room with a sense of finality. We finally knew what had been causing our princess so much distress, but the relief was short-lived. What followed was the stark realization that our world was about to change in ways we couldn't even fully comprehend.

The doctor explained that celiac disease is an autoimmune disorder in which the body's immune system attacks its own small intestine whenever gluten is ingested. Gluten, a protein found in wheat, barley, and rye, would trigger an immune response in her body, damaging the tiny hair-like structures in the small intestine that help absorb nutrients. Even the smallest trace of gluten could set off a cascade of harmful reactions. It wasn't just about making a few adjustments to her diet; it was a complete overhaul of how we approached food, meals, and every social gathering in our lives.

At that moment, we felt a strange combination of relief and fear. The endless questioning of what was wrong with our child, the frustration of not having any answers for so long, was finally over. But it was replaced by the gnawing fear of how this disease would affect her childhood, her future, and how we would navigate the world with this new reality.

As we sat quietly in the car on the ride home, our minds raced with questions and worries. Would she ever be able to enjoy birthday parties, family dinners, or school lunches in the same way? How would she feel when she saw her friends eating the foods she loved, knowing she couldn't have them? The uncertainty of it all seemed disturbing.

? Understanding Celiac Disease:

The hardest part of the entire process was breaking the news to our little girl. How do you explain to a child that some of her favourite foods—things she had loved for years—could now make her sick? Manviya was so full of life and excitement, and her love for sweet treats and baked goods was something we had always indulged. How could we tell her that cookies, cakes, and sandwiches would now have to be permanently off-limits?

We knew we had to be gentle but honest. As we sat down with her, we prepared ourselves to explain what celiac disease meant in simple, child-friendly terms. "Sweetheart," we began, "there's something important we need to talk to you about." Her big black eyes looked up at us with curiosity, sensing that something was different. "Your body has a condition called celiac disease, which means you can't eat foods like bread, cakes, cookies, or anything with gluten in it because it will make you sick."

We watched her face closely as we explained the cause and effect. The hardest moment was seeing her process the news. Her eyes widened slightly, and for a brief moment, her face reflected a mix of confusion and worry. How could she not be upset? How could a child as young as she was understand the full implications of such a diagnosis?

But then, she did something extraordinary. With the most innocent of smiles, she looked at us and said, "It's okay, Mommy and Daddy. We can make new favourites!"

In that moment, all our fears about how she would handle this change vanished. She wasn't scared. She wasn't upset. She had, in her childlike wisdom, already chosen to embrace this new reality with hope and optimism. Manviya wasn't focused on what she couldn't have; instead, she was thinking about what she could make and enjoy. Her words were like a balm for our hearts. It was as though she had given us permission to face this journey with the same courage and hope she had.

? The Emotional Impact:

In the days following the diagnosis, a whirlwind of emotions engulfed us. Relief was immediately followed by a sense of fear and uncertainty. As parents, we grappled with the many unknowns: How would this affect Manviya's future? How would she navigate a world with her celiac disease? Would she ever feel left out, or worse, isolated?

We feared the emotional impact on her. Would she be able to fully participate in birthday parties or school events? Would she ever be able to eat the same foods as her friends, or would she always feel different? The thought of her sitting at a birthday party, watching her friends enjoy cake while she ate something different, was heartbreaking. Would she feel sad, frustrated, or angry?

But then we looked at Manviya and saw the strength and courage she had already demonstrated. She was facing this with a resilience that took us by surprise. Yes, the challenges were real, and yes, they were daunting, but her optimism was unwavering. Her words, "We can make new favourites," kept ringing in our ears. They became our reminder that even in the face of difficulty, there is always room for hope and joy.

We realized that this journey wasn't just about avoiding gluten; it was about making sure Manviya's spirit remained as strong and joyful as ever. The emotional toll was real, but it was also a catalyst for change. We were no longer just concerned parents—we were advocates for our daughter's happiness, and we would do everything in our power to ensure she thrived, no matter the challenges.

? Breaking the News to Manviya:

Breaking the news to Manviya about her celiac disease was one of the hardest moments we've faced as parents. How do you tell a young child that her favorite cookies, cakes, and even bread could harm her? Sitting down together, our hearts were heavy. We gently explained that her body couldn't tolerate gluten and that eating it could make her very sick.

Her reaction took us by surprise. Her face fell briefly as she processed the information, but then, with a resilience beyond her years, she looked at us and said, "It's okay, Mommy and Daddy. We can make new favorites."

Her unexpected grace in that moment left us speechless. Instead of despair, she embraced the challenge with optimism. Her words became a beacon of hope for us, reminding us that even in the face of adversity, there is always room for creativity, love, and new beginnings.

From that moment on, Manviya led us with her courage and adventurous spirit. Rather than mourning the foods she could no longer have, she eagerly explored new possibilities. She approached her diagnosis not as a limitation but as an opportunity to find joy in creating new favourites.

Her resilience taught us that hardship isn't just something to endure—it's something to grow through. She showed us how to face challenges with hope and grace, proving that even the most difficult changes can bring about beautiful new opportunities. With her optimism lighting the way, we knew we could face anything together as a family.

? *The Family's Resolve:*

The diagnosis was not the end—it was the beginning of a new chapter in our family's journey. Yes, it was daunting, and yes, it would require immense effort and adjustment, but we were committed. We knew that every meal, every celebration, every outing would require planning, care, and attention. We would have to adjust, learn, and grow together. But through it all, one thing remained certain: we would ensure that Manviya's health and happiness would always come first.

We promised to stand by her, no matter what. We promised to make sure she never felt excluded, to celebrate her victories no matter how small, and to help her live a life filled with joy, even within the confines of her new reality. Together, as a family, we would create new traditions, new solutions, and a new sense of normal. And above all, we would do it together—with love, patience, and unwavering resolve.

This was not just about managing celiac disease. It was about reinforcing the foundation of our family—our strength, our unity, and our love for one another. With Manviya's resilience to guide us, we would navigate this new chapter with courage, finding joy and hope in every challenge we faced.

The diagnosis is just a moment in time. It didn't define us, and it certainly didn't define Manviya. What defined us is our commitment to her well-being and our collective resilience. We were a family that faced challenges together, a family that embraced the journey, no matter where it led.

CHAPTER FOUR

REDEFINING OUR WORLD

Redefining Our World:

The journey after Manviya's diagnosis of celiac disease felt like stepping into a completely new world—one that was filled with challenges we never anticipated. From the simple act of preparing meals to the seemingly mundane task of grocery shopping, every aspect of our lives needed to be carefully rethought, adapted, and restructured. What once felt easy and natural was now fraught with the complexity of ensuring that every decision we made would protect our little princess and keep her healthy.

? Transforming the Kitchen:

The kitchen was no longer just a place for family dinners and spontaneous cooking experiments. It had become the frontline of our battle against gluten, where we had to be vigilant at all times. Everything that we thought we knew about preparing food had to be reconsidered. We began by thoroughly assessing every single item in our kitchen. That old toaster, which had faithfully browned countless slices of bread, was suddenly deemed unsafe because of the potential gluten crumbs hiding within. Our cutting boards, pans, and utensils—everything had to be replaced. Gluten could lurk anywhere, and we weren't willing to take any risks.

At first, it felt overwhelming. The kitchen, once a place of joy and creativity, now seemed like a battleground. Cooking became an exact science, one that required precision, attention to detail, and a new set of rules. We made sure to designate specific areas for gluten-free food preparation and labelled containers for the ingredients we could safely use. It wasn't just about replacing items; it was about transforming the very space where we had once freely cooked into a fortress against contamination.

The process was slow, and mistakes were inevitable. We had to learn the hard way that a single crumb could have dire consequences for Manviya's health. We had to teach ourselves new cooking techniques, find new ways to get the texture and flavour we craved without gluten, and adjust to the fact that the spontaneous, carefree meals we once took for granted were no longer an option. But with each challenge, we found a way to make it work. We tried, we failed, and we tried again. Slowly, the kitchen became a space of empowerment, creativity, and shared love rather than fear and restriction.

Our princess, ever the optimist, was right there with us. She eagerly joined in, rolling out gluten-free dough with a smile on her face and taste-testing every new recipe we made. Her joy reminded us that this process wasn't about limitations—it was about coming together as a family, finding new ways to create special moments, and keeping the love and joy alive in the kitchen.

? Grocery Shopping Adventures:

Grocery shopping had once been a routine chore. We'd go in, grab what we needed, and be done. But now, every trip felt like embarking on a treasure hunt, where every item required scrutiny. Gluten was everywhere, hidden in sauces, condiments, and even candy. We quickly learned that shopping for groceries was no longer as simple as checking off a list—it was an exercise in vigilance and persistence.

Initially, the sheer volume of information was enough to make our heads spin. We'd scan ingredients lists, looking for the usual offenders like wheat, barley, and rye. But soon, we realized that gluten could hide in so many unexpected places. We had to learn the language of food labels—malt extract, modified food starch, natural flavours. These terms, once meaningless to us, became red flags we couldn't ignore. Each trip was an education in itself, and it often felt like we were learning as we went, making mistakes and adjusting as we became more knowledgeable.

There were moments of frustration—foods we had always trusted suddenly became off-limits, and the sheer number of gluten-free options on the market only added to the confusion. Some gluten-free products were excellent, while others were more akin to cardboard than food. The first loaf of gluten-free bread we tried could have been used as a paperweight, and the gluten-free crackers we bought crumbled into pieces at the slightest touch. But we persevered. We laughed at our mishaps, learned from our mistakes, and slowly began to fill our pantry with items that worked for us.

As we grew more experienced, our grocery shopping trips became smoother and more efficient. We developed detailed shopping lists, categorized by store sections, and started recognizing brands and products that we trusted. The bright gluten-free labels became familiar sights, and trips to specialty shops or farmers' markets for gluten-free items became part of the fun. Grocery shopping, once a chore, turned into an empowering experience. We began to see it not as a task filled with limitations but as a way to discover new and exciting options for our family.

And even more than that, our little princess made the process enjoyable. She would enthusiastically point out gluten-free products on the shelves, helping us pick out snacks and treats. Her joy turned a seemingly burdensome task into something that brought us closer together and filled us with excitement for what we could try next.

? The Challenges of Dining Out:

Dining out had always been a treasured family tradition, a time to share stories and laughter over a delicious meal. But everything changed when our daughter, Manviya, was diagnosed with celiac disease. What once felt effortless now seemed like a daunting challenge. Could we trust restaurants to truly understand the seriousness of a gluten-free diet? Would we be seen as overly demanding or, worse, ignored altogether?

At first, we hesitated to speak up, unsure of how to navigate this new reality. Asking too many questions felt awkward, and we didn't want to draw attention. But as we learned more about celiac disease, we realized there was no room for compromise. Keeping Manviya safe meant putting her health above all else, even if it meant stepping outside our comfort zone.

We began by educating ourselves about what to ask when dining out. "Do you have a dedicated gluten-free menu?" "How do you avoid cross-contamination?" "Is your staff trained to handle gluten-free requests?" These questions became our compass, guiding us through what initially felt like a minefield. Many times, the answers we received were not reassuring. Some restaurants didn't understand the complexities of gluten-free dining, and others couldn't guarantee a safe meal. In those moments, we often left, choosing caution over risk.

Eventually, we started bringing homemade gluten-free meals or snacks for her, a decision that ensured her safety while allowing us to enjoy the outing as a family. Identifying restaurants that genuinely understood celiac disease was rare, but every discovery felt like finding a gem. Hope one-day pioneer establishments served gluten-free meals with care, and those will become our go-to spots.

Even with our precautions, there were moments of uncertainty. A garnish on a plate would look suspicious, or a server's hesitance would make us question the kitchen's protocols. During such times, our fallback plan—a stash of gluten-free snacks—proved invaluable. These small steps helped us navigate tricky situations.

Throughout it all, her cheerful spirit kept us going. "It's okay, Mommy and Daddy," she would say with a smile. "I like my snacks just as much." Her optimism turned what could have been a burden into a shared family mission. It reminded us that while dining out required more effort, it didn't have to feel overwhelming.

With time and persistence, we grew more confident in advocating for her needs. We will learn to recognize which restaurants took gluten-free dining seriously and gradually built a network of safe options.

? Building a Network of Safe Options:

Discovering a network of trusted gluten-free restaurants will be an exciting yet challenging journey. It will demand patience, persistence, and a willingness to embrace trial and error. Initially, we might encounter places that claim to offer gluten-free options but don't fully understand the importance of preventing cross-contamination. Those early disappointments will likely test our resolve, but they will also drive our determination.

In time, we'll begin identifying restaurants, bakeries, and cafes that genuinely prioritize gluten-free dining. This journey won't just be about ensuring safety; it will be about rediscovering the joy of sharing meals as a family. Slowly but surely, our efforts are bound to bear fruit. We'll uncover bakeries serving mouthwatering gluten-free pastries, pizza places with dedicated kitchens, and ice cream parlors that cater exclusively to gluten-free needs.

As we navigate this journey, we'll remember why it matters so much. It won't just be about finding safe food—it will be about creating moments of connection, joy, and family bonding. Though the path may seem daunting, every step forward will strengthen our confidence and open new doors to safe and happy dining experiences.

? Adapting as a Family:

Celiac disease didn't just change the way we ate—it changed the way we lived. Our routines, habits, and even our outlook on life were reshaped in the wake of this diagnosis. But through it all, we stood united as a family, determined to protect Manviya's health while ensuring that our home remained a place of joy, love, and safety.

Every part of our daily life was impacted. Meal preparation became a shared responsibility, with each family member learning to cook gluten-free meals. Together, we experimented with new recipes, trying to recreate some of our old favourites while discovering new dishes that became staples in our home. Each successful experiment felt like a small victory—a triumph of creativity, resilience, and love.

Outside the kitchen, our routines changed as well. Holidays, birthdays, and special events—occasions that once revolved around food—became opportunities to get creative and plan ahead. We packed gluten-free snacks for Manviya, ensuring she wouldn't feel left out at parties or school events. We spoke with friends, teachers, and family members, helping them understand her needs and educating them on how they could make small adjustments to accommodate her.

The road wasn't always easy. There were moments of frustration and confusion, especially when explaining why certain foods couldn't be shared or when navigating family gatherings where the risk of cross-contamination was higher. But with patience, humour, and determination, we adapted.

We learned that true happiness doesn't come from the food we eat but from the love and laughter we share. Movie nights, picnics, and family game nights became treasured traditions, reminding us that, even with dietary restrictions, we could still enjoy life's simple pleasures.

? The Journey to Empowerment:

At first, the journey felt overwhelming. Fear and confusion clouded our minds as we grappled with the implications of Manviya's diagnosis. Would we be able to navigate this new reality without feeling defeated? Would we ever truly adjust?

But as time passed, fear transformed into determination. With each challenge, we grew stronger. We educated ourselves, leaned on others who had walked the same path, and found support in the community of families facing similar struggles. We began to understand that celiac disease wasn't just something we had to manage—it was a chance to empower ourselves and to grow as a family.

Our journey wasn't just about avoiding gluten; it was about redefining what it meant to be a family. We learned to adapt, to find joy in the unexpected, and to face challenges with resilience. And, through it all, our love for Manviya remained our guiding force, reminding us that, as long as we faced this journey together, there was nothing we couldn't overcome.

While the road ahead will still have its hurdles, we now know one thing for sure: we will continue to face every challenge with love, strength, and unwavering determination. Celiac disease may have changed our world, but it will never diminish the love that holds our family together. Together, we are stronger than any obstacle that comes our way.

CHAPTER FIVE

THE SOCIAL STRUGGLE

The Social Struggle: Social events such as birthday parties, school celebrations, and family gatherings are supposed to be times of joy and laughter, but for us, they became bittersweet milestones. They were constant reminders of the limitations celiac disease imposed on our precious girl, our princess. We watched her eyes linger on the cakes, snacks, and treats that her friends enjoyed with carefree abandon. She, with her radiant smile, would often mask her disappointment, choosing not to draw attention to herself. But there were times when her eyes betrayed her, showing the sadness she worked so hard to conceal. It was heart-wrenching to witness this struggle. The experience of watching her friends indulge in things she couldn't have been a constant reminder of how different her world was becoming.

However, we were determined not to let these moments of longing define her childhood. We set out to make sure that our princess didn't feel left out. At every event, we worked tirelessly to create gluten-free alternatives, ensuring that she could enjoy the festivities just as much as her peers. It wasn't just about providing substitutes for the treats her friends ate—it was about ensuring that she always felt included, never singled out. With each cupcake we baked, every muffin we packed, and every special snack we brought to her school, we made sure that she could participate without feeling the weight of her restrictions.

Yet, despite our best efforts, there were still difficult moments. There were days when she would ask, "Why can't I have what they're having?" Her innocent question would tug at our hearts, and it took every ounce of strength not to let our emotions drain us. We gently explained that her health was the reason for her dietary restrictions. It became our mission to make sure she understood that her health was our top priority, even if it meant missing out on certain treats.

In those moments of sadness, we also witnessed something beautiful: a change in her. Over time, she began to understand, not only the "why" behind her diet, but also how to navigate these social situations. She began to embrace her uniqueness, and we could see the transformation in her. The shift wasn't just within her—it extended outward as well. Her teachers, classmates, and their families rallied around her, becoming pillars of support. Slowly but surely, the environment that once felt isolating became a community of inclusion and love. Her classmates started asking questions, and her teachers ensured that her school environment was always safe. What started as a difficult struggle evolved into a powerful journey of inclusion, education, and love.

? The Challenges of Social Events:

As we adjusted to our new reality, it became clear that social events were going to be challenging for all of us. They were no longer the simple, carefree moments of the past. Now, each birthday party, marriage celebration, reception, holiday gathering, or school celebration was accompanied by a sense of both excitement and apprehension. Our princess would look at the birthday cakes, the cookies, and the candy, knowing she could not partake in those treats. The weight of her dietary restrictions often hung heavy in the air.

It wasn't just about her not being able to eat the same things as the other kids; it was about the feeling of being "different." Social events should have been a time for carefree fun, yet they often became a source of quiet disappointment. She'd smile and play with her friends, but you could tell she was trying to be brave. We watched as her face lit up when she saw a gluten-free treat on the table, but the struggle to maintain composure was always there.

We realized early on that the key to making these social events easier was not to avoid them but to face them head-on, with creativity and preparation. We started making gluten-free alternatives for every occasion. Birthday parties, school gatherings, or family celebrations no longer required us to sit on the sidelines. We brought our own cakes, cupcakes, and cookies, decorated just as beautifully as any traditional treat. We ensured that our princess could have a slice of cake at the party or a snack during a school event, just like everyone else.

? Creating Gluten-Free Alternatives:

As the realization set in that our princess would not be able to eat many of the treats offered at social events, we began to take matters into our own hands. Our mission was clear: we would create a world where she could enjoy every moment without feeling deprived. We became experts in gluten-free cooking and baking—researching recipes, experimenting with ingredients, and even attending gluten-free cooking classes to make sure our treats were not only safe but also delicious.

It was through these trials that we found the joy of cooking and baking together as a family. Birthday parties became opportunities for us to be creative. Instead of simply picking up a gluten-free cake from a bakery, we learned to bake her favourite cakes and cookies ourselves. We made everything from decadent chocolate chip cookies to moist cakes adorned with colourful frosting, so our princess could join in the celebration without missing a beat.

At school, we packed her favourite gluten-free snacks—homemade laddu, Chikki, muffins, and fruit-filled treats. The idea wasn't just about providing a substitute, but about creating a sense of normalcy for her. With every snack we brought to school, we were affirming that she was just as much a part of the experience as anyone else.

It wasn't always easy—there were times when we felt frustrated by the endless cooking and baking sessions, or when we worried whether the snacks, we brought would be good enough. But the joy on our princess's face when she could sit at the table with her friends and enjoy a treat, laughing and chatting as though she wasn't any different, made every effort worth it.

? Educating Teachers and Peers:

As we navigated these social events, we realized that providing gluten-free alternatives was only part of the solution. We also needed to educate those around our princess—her teachers, friends, and their families. Without this critical understanding, our efforts to create a safe and supportive environment for her would not be enough. It was time to build a foundation of awareness.

We approached her teachers and school staff with the hope of educating them about celiac disease. We explained how even the smallest trace of gluten could cause harm and why it was essential for her to have safe food options at all school events, from class parties to field trips. Fortunately, her teachers were receptive, and they worked hard to make sure she was always included and kept safe.

But we didn't stop there. We also wanted to reach her classmates. We spoke to the class in a fun, engaging way, using visuals and simple explanations about celiac disease. We even had a gluten-free snack day, where the children could sample some of the treats our princess enjoyed. To our delight, the kids were not only curious but excited to help. They began asking questions and showing empathy toward our daughter's dietary needs.

We didn't stop at the school either. We also reached out to the parents of her friends, encouraging them to learn about celiac disease and how they could help. When we started receiving invitations to play-dates or birthday parties, we would take the time to talk with the parents about what foods were safe and what they could do to make sure Manviya didn't feel excluded.

The effort paid off. We started seeing changes in the way her classmates treated her. They offered to play games with her when snacks were being passed around, or even asked if they could bring gluten-free treats to a gathering just for her. This support was nothing short of heart-warming. It was clear that we weren't just teaching the children about a medical condition—we were fostering a culture of empathy and inclusion that extended far beyond our family.

? Fostering Inclusion:

For us, the goal was simple: we wanted our princess to feel included. We didn't want her to feel as though she was on the outside looking in while her friends' enjoyed treats and celebrations. But inclusion wasn't just about giving her gluten-free snacks; it was about creating a culture where she could thrive without feeling like she was any different.

We worked tirelessly to create this environment, starting with her teachers and classmates. We organized special events, like school parties, where everyone could enjoy gluten-free treats. Instead of separating her from the rest of the group, we made sure that everyone had access to gluten-free options. We even hosted gluten-free cooking sessions at home, inviting her friends to come and bake cookies and cakes together. These sessions not only made learning about celiac disease fun but also allowed her friends to be actively involved in creating treats that everyone could enjoy.

Over time, the effort to create an inclusive environment paid off. Manviya's classmates began to see her dietary needs as just another part of who she was. They stopped viewing her as the girl with dietary restrictions and started embracing her for her unique personality. The simple act of including her in food-related activities transformed her experience. It allowed her to feel empowered and proud of whom she was, rather than feeling isolated or different.

? Lessons in Resilience:

Through these challenges, we were determined to in still in Manviya not just the ability to cope with her condition but to thrive despite it. We wanted her to understand that having celiac disease didn't make her any less of a person; it simply meant that she had to navigate the world differently.

We taught her about resilience—not as a way to deny her feelings of frustration or sadness, but as a tool to face those emotions with strength and grace. We made sure she knew that it was okay to feel upset when she couldn't have the same foods as her friends. We also encouraged her to speak up for herself, whether it was explaining her dietary needs to a friend or reminding a teacher about what foods were safe for her to eat.

As she grew, Manviya's resilience became a beacon of strength for all of us. We watched as she learned to embrace her uniqueness, using it as a source of pride rather than something to be ashamed of. She became a confident young girl who not only adapted to her condition but also flourished. She was no longer defined by her disease—she was defined by her character, her kindness, and her incredible strength.

? Moments of Triumph:

Amid the challenges, we experienced moments of triumph that filled our hearts with pride. One of the most memorable moments was at a birthday party when we didn't need to bring her own gluten-free snacks. The host, who had learned about celiac disease, had arranged some certified gluten-free options alongside the regular food. Watching Manviya walk into that party with a big smile on her face, knowing she could partake in the treats just like everyone else, was a victory that we had worked so hard for.

These moments of triumph, while small, were symbolic of the progress we had made. It wasn't just about the gluten-free cake—it was about inclusion, empathy, and love. Our daughter was no longer seen as different but as a valuable and loved member of her community. And that, above all else, was our ultimate victory.

? Strengthening Bonds:

Through all of the struggles and triumphs, we found that the challenges of navigating celiac disease helped to strengthen the bonds within our family. Every meal we planned, every social gathering we attended, and every gluten-free treat we baked became a shared experience. Our family grew closer, learning to support one another in ways we never had before.

As we shared our journey with others, we saw how our community began to rally around us. Friends, teachers, and even strangers began to embrace our mission. They didn't just learn about celiac disease—they learned about empathy, inclusion, and support. Our journey with celiac disease became not just about managing a health condition but about creating a ripple effect of kindness and understanding in our community.

In the end, it became clear that the true strength of our family lies not just in how we navigated challenges, but in how we came together, supported each other, and ultimately thrived. Through it all, we learned that the greatest triumph wasn't simply about overcoming obstacles—it was about doing so together, as a family, as a community, and with love.

CHAPTER SIX

FINDING COMMUNITY – A NEW NORMAL

Our journey with Manviya's diagnosis was a challenge like no other. It often felt as though we were sailing on a small boat, tossed by the waves of confusion, frustration, and fear. But amidst this turbulence, there was a constant beacon of hope that guided us forward: the discovery of community. In this new world, we weren't alone. We had found other families who understood, supported, and shared the weight of living with celiac disease. As we began to connect, something beautiful started to emerge—a sense of belonging, a network of families walking similar paths, each one offering strength, advice, and love.

? The Search for Support:

In the early days following Manviya's diagnosis, we were overwhelmed. We knew very little about celiac disease and felt as though we were venturing into the unknown. It was a time of learning, of changing our habits, and of being constantly vigilant about what we ate, where we went, and even who we trusted with our daughter's well-being. At times, it felt like we were sailing in the dark, without a map or compass.

But as time passed, we realized that while we may have been on an unfamiliar journey, we were not alone. There was a world of people out there who understood our struggles and our triumphs—families like ours, parents like us, who had faced the same challenges and had stories to tell. We didn't have to learn everything from scratch. There was a wealth of wisdom in these communities, and it was available to us if we sought it.

Our search began online, where we discovered forums dedicated to celiac disease. These virtual spaces were filled with people who were eager to share their experiences, offer advice, and support one another. At first, we were hesitant to open up. But slowly, as we read through stories from others who had been where we were, we started to feel a sense of connection. These stories were not just about food restrictions or medical protocols. They were about real lives, real families, navigating the ups and downs of daily life with celiac disease. It was in these stories that we first realized that we were part of something larger than ourselves—a global community bound together by shared experiences and collective strength.

We began to read about others' victories in navigating social events, their tricks for meal planning, and the ways they had learned to manage birthday parties, holidays, and outings—all of which felt daunting in the beginning. There were also stories of setbacks and frustrations, but these too were comforting. They reminded us that it wasn't always easy, and that it was okay to struggle. There was no perfect path, no one-size-fits-all solution, but we didn't have to face these challenges alone. There was support, and it was just a few clicks away.

? Sharing Stories and Advice:

As we ventured deeper into these forums and connected with more families, we began to notice a remarkable shift in our own outlook. It wasn't just about surviving this new reality—it was about thriving, about finding joy and strength in the midst of our struggles. We began to see the power of shared knowledge. It wasn't just about the practical tips on navigating life with celiac disease, though those were invaluable. It was about the emotional support that came with hearing others say, "I've been there too," or, "This is what worked for us."

The most powerful moments came when we realized how much we had in common with others who had faced similar challenges. Meal planning, at first a daunting task, became manageable as we learned from families who had already made the transition to a gluten-free life. Parents shared their go-to recipes, their favourite brands, and even the tricks they had learned for making meals that were both delicious and safe. These exchanges helped us create a repertoire of recipes that were not only gluten-free but also enjoyable for the whole family, not just Manviya.

Social events, which had once been a source of stress, became more manageable as we picked up tips from others on how to navigate restaurants, birthday parties, and school activities. One parent suggested bringing along a special gluten-free treat for our child to ensure she never felt left out at parties, while others offered insights into how to manage eating out without the fear of cross-contamination. These conversations turned what felt like an overwhelming challenge into something that, while still requiring effort, was completely manageable.

We soon realized that these forums were more than just spaces for exchanging information—they were lifelines. They allowed us to share our own experiences, too. We offered advice on navigating school lunches and dealing with insensitive remarks from well-meaning friends and family. By sharing our story, we became part of the solution, helping others feel empowered and supported just as we had been.

? The Power of Shared Knowledge:

As we became more involved in these communities, we began to see the true power of shared knowledge. It was a resource like no other—a collection of wisdom and experience that had been honed over years of trial and error. From the practical to the emotional, the community's shared knowledge helped us in ways we never anticipated.

We learned about the hidden sources of gluten in everyday products, items we would never have thought to check. We discovered which brands offered the safest options, and which ones had built a reputation for catering specifically to celiac needs. Recipes that we thought were lost forever became accessible once more. Foods we had longed for—baked goods, pastas, pizzas—were suddenly available in a gluten-free version, thanks to the creativity of others.

What was perhaps most empowering was the knowledge we gained about the disease itself. The more we learned about celiac disease—about gluten's impact on the body and the importance of cross-contamination—the more confident we felt. We no longer felt as though we were merely reacting to the disease. We became active participants in managing it, equipped with the tools and understanding needed to navigate its challenges.

In sharing our own discoveries and resources, we too contributed to this vast pool of knowledge. Each family's unique perspective added another layer of understanding, and with it, a greater sense of solidarity. The knowledge shared in these communities wasn't just about managing celiac disease; it was about empowerment. It was about taking control of our lives, our health, and our future.

? Building Friendships:

One of the most beautiful aspects of this community was the friendships it helped to build. For Manviya, the connections she made with other children who had celiac disease were a source of great comfort. She had always been a bright, joyful child, but her diagnosis had left her feeling isolated at times. No longer was she the only one who couldn't eat certain foods or attend birthday parties without worrying about cross-contamination. She found friends who understood her, who shared her experiences, and who offered her a sense of belonging that had been missing for so long.

For us, as parents, these friendships offered something equally important: solidarity. We were not alone in our efforts. Just as Manviya had found friends, we found a network of parents who offered us emotional support, practical advice, and a deep understanding of what it meant to raise a child with celiac disease. Whether it was swapping tips on dealing with school lunches or offering encouragement during tough times, these friendships became a lifeline.

? Support beyond the Family:

While our family remained the core of our support system, the extended community we had found soon became equally vital. These were people who truly understood the emotional weight of managing celiac disease. They weren't just offering advice—they were offering empathy, validation, and a sense of camaraderie that made all the difference.

In many ways, our community became like a second family. They celebrated our victories, no matter how small, and offered words of comfort when things didn't go as planned. They were there during the difficult moments, reminding us that we weren't alone, and offering a helping hand when we needed it most. Through them, we found a renewed sense of hope. Together, we shared the burden and celebrated the triumphs.

? The Strength of a Community:

Through it all, one truth became clear: there is an unparalleled strength in community. It was through this network of families, friends, and supporters that we found the resilience to keep going, even on the toughest days. This strength wasn't just practical—it was emotional. In moments of doubt or frustration, we knew we could turn to our community for advice, encouragement, and simply a listening ear.

The collective wisdom we had gained from others became the foundation of our new normal. We had learned how to manage celiac disease, not just as a medical condition, but as part of our lives. We had found joy in our new reality, thanks to the support of the community that had lifted us up when we needed it most.

? Creating a New Normal:

Living with celiac disease was never going to be easy. But with each passing day, we adjusted. We adapted. We found ways to not only survive but to thrive. The key to this transformation lay in the community that had supported us along the way. Through online forums, local support groups, and friendships forged in the fire of shared experiences, we had found a new normal—one that was rich with hope, love, and a sense of belonging.

Together, we had created a world where Manviya could be a child, where she could laugh, play, and grow, just like any other child, despite the challenges of celiac disease. And in that, we found peace. Not because the road ahead would always be easy, but because we knew we didn't have to walk it alone.

? Hope and Healing: As we navigated the challenges of living with celiac disease, one of the most profound gifts the community gave us is not just practical support, but emotional healing. In the midst of the uncertainty and frustration that often accompanied our journey, we found solace in knowing we weren't alone. The stories shared by other families, their victories and struggles, resonated deeply with us. Their understanding and empathy allowed us to feel seen and heard, providing a kind of emotional comfort that words alone could not offer.

It isn't just about advice or recipes; it is about the collective strength we felt when we realized there were others who truly understood the weight of what we were going through. Every conversation, every shared experience, reinforced the belief that we were part of something bigger—something that isn't just about surviving celiac disease, but about thriving in spite of it. It is a reminder that the emotional and mental burden of our journey didn't have to be carried alone. The community's support gave us strength and resilience that we couldn't have found on our own.

In those tough moments, when fear or doubt threatened to overshadow our hope, the community's unwavering encouragement is a beacon of light. We came to understand that healing isn't just physical—it is emotional too. The power of shared understanding, the kindness of those who had walked this path before us, gave us the hope that no matter what challenges celiac disease presented, we could face them with courage and unity.

Together, we embraced a mindset of hope, knowing that each obstacle we encountered is one we could overcome, not in isolation, but as part of a strong, supportive network. The collective strength of the community helped us heal in ways we never expected, transforming our journey from one of fear and uncertainty into one of empowerment and hope. With each day, we felt more capable of meeting the challenges ahead, knowing that we had the support of others who truly understood our story.

CHAPTER SEVEN

THE SILVER LININGS

Celiac disease arrived in our lives like an uninvited storm. It was sudden, powerful, and left us reeling, unsure of what our next step would be. However, as the days and weeks passed, we came to realize that it was not just a challenge but also an opportunity—an opportunity for growth, reflection, and deeper connection as a family. Little did we know that this diagnosis would transform not only our daughter's life but also ours in ways we never imagined? The experience revealed unexpected lessons and forged a strength in us that would become the foundation of our new way of living.

? Unexpected Lessons:

Celiac disease did not arrive with an instruction manual. There was no clear roadmap, no simple path forward, and certainly no quick fixes. We found ourselves stumbling in the dark, learning on the go, and doing everything we could to make sure our daughter, Manviya, felt safe and supported. At first, the changes felt like an overwhelming burden. We had to sift through ingredient labels, make sense of medical jargon, and suddenly feel like experts in a field we had no prior knowledge of. Gluten became the enemy in our kitchen, in our meals, in our celebrations, and even in our social gatherings.

But with time, we began to see things differently. We understood that this wasn't just a challenge—it was an invitation for growth, not just for Manviya but for all of us. We began to embrace the changes, learning to adapt to a new rhythm of life. We no longer saw celiac disease as a threat, but as a catalyst for positive change. Our family, once scattered in the hustle of everyday life, began to grow closer, united by a common purpose: to protect and nurture our daughter. We found ourselves becoming better listeners, more patient with each other, and more aware of the small moments that mattered the most.

In the beginning, it seemed like a never-ending battle against gluten. Every meal felt like a test, every grocery trips a scavenger hunt for safe ingredients. But, as we spent more time in the kitchen together, something beautiful began to unfold. We discovered new recipes, explored new cuisines, and began to appreciate food in a way we never had before. The kitchen, which had once been a place of routine, became a place of creativity and experimentation.

Manviya, in her own quiet way, taught us more than we could have imagined. Despite the challenges she faced, she handled her diagnosis with grace, strength, and a level of maturity far beyond her years. Instead of feeling defeated by the restrictions, she embraced them. She took to gluten-free cooking and baking with enthusiasm, turning what seemed like a limitation into a source of joy. Watching her experiment with new recipes, trying her hand at gluten-free cakes and cookies, brought us all a sense of pride and wonder.

More than just creating treats, she taught us all the importance of perseverance. When a batch of cookies didn't turn out right, she didn't give up—she learned from it and tried again. In her joy of cooking and baking, we saw not only her resilience but her creativity, and that became a model for all of us. Through Manviya's eyes, we realized that every challenge was an opportunity to grow, to become more creative, more patient, and more compassionate.

? Strengthened Family Bonds:
The journey that started with Manviya's diagnosis became more than just a series of medical and dietary adjustments—it became the heart of our family's evolution. The changes weren't just about food; they were about the way we saw each other, how we communicated, and how we worked together as a unit. It was not just about managing her health condition—it was about building a deeper connection that would last long after the initial shock of the diagnosis had worn off.

The transition to a gluten-free lifestyle was a process of trial and error, filled with moments of frustration, fear, and uncertainty. There were days when the weight of it all felt too heavy to bear—the worry of hidden gluten in unexpected places, the stress of trying to find safe foods when dining out, and the anxiety of making sure we never made a mistake in our food preparation. We found ourselves questioning everything, double-checking labels, and always being vigilant.

But through it all, we leaned on each other. What could have driven us apart—stress, fatigue, frustration—actually brought us closer. We realized that we weren't just adjusting Manviya's diet; we were adapting our entire lifestyle. Every meal was an act of love, every decision about food a collective choice. We worked together, supported one another, and celebrated each victory, no matter how small. And slowly, the strain that could have divided us turned into a bond that strengthened our family.

There were moments when the challenge of managing her condition seemed insurmountable, but those moments were far outweighed by the beauty of watching our family come together. We were no longer simply a group of individuals living under one roof; we became a team, united in our purpose and our love for one another. The journey wasn't easy, but it was transformative. And through it, we found new ways to connect, support, and love each other.

Manviya's resilience was a beacon of strength. Her determination to face each challenge with a smile, her enthusiasm for cooking and baking gluten-free treats, and her ability to bring lightness and joy into even the most difficult moments inspired us all. Her strength became the anchor that held us steady through the storm.

? Healthier Eating Habits:

One of the most significant changes that came from Manviya's celiac diagnosis was the transformation of our family's approach to food. Initially, the shift to a gluten-free diet felt restrictive, even daunting. We had to re-think our entire approach to shopping, meal planning, and cooking. The idea of finding safe ingredients seemed overwhelming. But as we navigated this new world, we began to see that these changes were not just about avoiding gluten—they were about embracing a healthier, more mindful way of eating.

Our diet gradually shifted from pre-packaged and processed foods to fresh, whole ingredients. No longer did we rely on quick fixes or convenience foods; instead, we began to cook more from scratch. Fresh fruits, vegetables, lean proteins, and gluten-free grains became the cornerstone of our meals. Our dinners became more colourful, more nourishing, and, over time, we noticed a significant improvement in our overall health.

The most profound change wasn't just in the food itself, but in the way we thought about food. We began to ask ourselves more intentional questions about what we were eating, not just for Manviya's sake but for all of us. We thought about the nutritional value of every ingredient, the way food made us feel, and the importance of eating together as a family. It became about more than just filling our bellies—it became about nourishing our bodies, minds, and spirits.

Through this shift in our eating habits, we discovered that gluten-free eating didn't mean sacrificing flavour or enjoyment. In fact, it opened the door to new culinary experiences. We found ourselves experimenting with new ingredients, trying new recipes, and discovering flavours we had never considered before. This new way of cooking didn't just help us keep Manviya safe—it brought us closer, united in the joy of preparing meals together.

Perhaps the greatest gift of this transformation was how it impacted our overall health. We all started to feel better. We had more energy, better digestion, and even noticed improvements in our skin. What began as a dietary necessity for Manviya had become a lifestyle change that benefitted everyone in the family. We became more attuned to our bodies and more mindful of the food that sustained us.

? Discovering New Passions:

One of the unexpected joys of living with celiac disease was watching Manviya discover a new passion for gluten-free cooking and baking. Initially, cooking and baking was a necessity—a way to ensure that she had safe treats to enjoy. But it quickly became more than that. Cooking and baking became a space for her to explore her creativity, express herself, and gain a sense of independence.

Her interest in cooking and baking began innocently enough. She started by asking questions—about ingredients, about the process, and about the art of making something from scratch. We welcomed her curiosity, showing her how to measure ingredients, mix doughs, and use the oven safely. Soon, she wanted to take over. She experimented with different gluten-free flours, tried out new combinations of flavors, and even began developing her own frosting recipes.

Cooking and baking became her outlet for creativity. It was no longer just about following recipes—it was about finding her own voice in the kitchen. Every successful batch of cookies or cupcakes filled her with pride. And every failure was an opportunity to learn and improve. Through it all, she found not only a sense of accomplishment but a deeper connection to her health journey. Cooking and baking gave her a way to embrace her condition and turn it into something beautiful.

But it wasn't just about cooking and baking—it was about the joy of creating something from scratch, of turning a simple set of ingredients into something delicious and meaningful. Manviya's gluten-free treats weren't just a reflection of her talent—they were a symbol of her resilience, her adaptability, and her ability to turn challenges into opportunities.

? Pride in Progress:

The pride we felt as we watched Manviya with her father bake her gluten-free treats was immeasurable. Each tray of freshly baked cookies, each perfect swirl of frosting, and every soft, pillowy muffin that came out of the oven felt like a victory—not just for her but for all of us. In the beginning, her gluten-free creations were a little rough around the edges, but with time and practice, they became more refined, more delicious, and more of a testament to her determination.

Cooking and baking had become Mr. and Mrs. Singh's personal expression along with Manviya, a way for her to show the world that, despite her diagnosis, she was thriving. The sense of pride we felt as parents wasn't just in the end result but in the process itself. We marvelled at her persistence, her patience, and her ability to adapt and learn.

What began as a simple necessity had turned into something extraordinary. Manviya's progress in the kitchen, her growing skills, and her unwavering enthusiasm reminded us that even in the face of adversity, there is room for growth, joy, and creativity. As we shared our treats with friends, family, and classmates, we couldn't help but feel a sense of pride in the way she had turned her challenges into a celebration of her own resilience. Each time we sat down to enjoy one of her treats, we were reminded of the strength of our family and the beautiful, silver lining that had emerged from the storm.

Through Manviya's gluten-free journey, we learned that challenges are not always obstacles—they are opportunities to grow, to connect, and to find new ways to thrive. And in every small victory, every sweet treat, and every moment of joy, we were reminded that even the hardest of trials can lead to the most beautiful of transformations.

CHAPTER EIGHT

ADVOCATING FOR AWARENESS

As we embarked on our journey with Manviya, the most unexpected challenge wasn't just navigating the physical aspects of celiac disease but encountering the startling lack of awareness surrounding it. It was disheartening to discover how little the world understood this condition, especially when it came to how severe the risks of gluten exposure are for those living with celiac disease. Whether it was at a restaurant, a school, or even among friends and family, we often found ourselves in situations where people didn't fully grasp the gravity of the disease. Too many, it seemed like a mere dietary preference, something manageable or avoidable—but for us, it was a life-threatening condition that demanded constant vigilance.

We knew that something had to change. We couldn't afford to let ignorance put Manviya's health at risk. So, we took it upon ourselves to advocate for awareness, to educate others on the seriousness of gluten exposure, and to ensure that no one misunderstood the importance of preventing cross-contamination. This mission became our guiding force, propelling us forward even when the road seemed impossibly difficult.

? Raising Awareness About Celiac Disease:

Our first lesson in advocacy came when we realized just how little the world understood about celiac disease. For many, the word "gluten-free" was nothing more than a trendy diet choice, something that could be easily accommodated at a restaurant or a social gathering. But the reality was starkly different. For people like Manviya, a single crumb of gluten could trigger severe and life-threatening reactions. That's when we understood the depth of the challenge before us—not just managing Manviya's disease but educating others about its risks.

Dining out became a frequent battleground for us. We would sit down at a restaurant, and the staff would often assure us that they could prepare gluten-free meals. But all too often, it became clear that they didn't understand the critical nature of preventing cross-contamination. A gluten-free meal wasn't just about using gluten-free ingredients; it was about making sure that every tool, surface, and process involved was free of any gluten traces. The misunderstanding of these crucial points often left us feeling vulnerable and on edge.

So, we decided to take matters into our own hands. We began advocating and educating those around us—restaurants, schools, and our circle of friends and family—about the true nature of celiac disease. We started small, having one-on-one conversations with waitstaff, teachers, and even family members. We explained that for us, it wasn't just about avoiding gluten; it was about preventing it from entering Manviya's body in any form. A single exposure could cause damage that would take months to heal, and the consequences were much more severe than people realized.

Each conversation felt like a small victory, and gradually, we began to see the impact of our efforts. Our aim wasn't just to make our lives easier—it was to create a world where others with celiac disease wouldn't have to fight for the safety they deserved. Every step we took felt like we were laying the foundation for a safer, more informed future.

? Educating Restaurants and Food Establishments:

One of the most frustrating and frequent challenges we faced in our journey was dining out. While it may seem like a simple pleasure, it was anything but for us. Many restaurants proudly offered gluten-free options, but most didn't understand the significance of preventing cross-contamination. A separate cooking space, different utensils, and a commitment to thoroughly cleaning surfaces were crucial to ensuring safety. Yet, too often, these basic precautions were overlooked.

In the beginning, we didn't know how to approach the subject. But we quickly realized that if we wanted to ensure Manviya's safety, we had to be proactive. We started talking to restaurant owners, chefs, and wait staff, explaining the seriousness of cross-contamination and the specific precautions that needed to be taken. We made sure to emphasize that it wasn't just about offering a gluten-free meal—it was about taking responsibility for every step in the cooking process to avoid any trace of gluten.

Some restaurants were dismissive or indifferent, which was incredibly frustrating, but others listened. Slowly, we began to see changes. Certain establishments started designating gluten-free spaces in their kitchens, investing in separate utensils, and adopting better cleaning practices. Each restaurant that took the time to understand and implement these changes was a win, not just for Manviya but for the entire community of people living with Gluten medical conditions.

The process wasn't always easy or fast, but it was worth it. These victories, though small, created a ripple effect in the dining community, and we were hopeful that this advocacy would one day make eating out a safer experience for everyone with celiac disease.

? Educating Schools and Teachers:

Our advocacy didn't stop with restaurants. As we navigated life with Manviya, we quickly realized that schools—where she spent a significant portion of her day—also lacked the necessary knowledge to keep her safe. We were shocked to learn that many teachers, cafeteria workers, and even school nurses weren't fully equipped to handle the dietary needs of a child with celiac disease. While schools were often well-meaning, the potential risks of cross-contamination were high, and we couldn't afford to take any chances.

We began by meeting with teachers, the school nurse, and cafeteria staff to explain the severity of the condition. We shared how even the smallest exposure to gluten could trigger a harmful reaction. But we didn't stop there. We worked with the school to create a safe, supportive environment for Manviya. We advocated for designated snack times where gluten-free options were available, and for a safe, gluten-free space for her to enjoy her food, free from the risk of cross-contamination.

The school was initially uncertain, but over time, we saw a shift. The teachers took the time to learn about celiac disease, and many of them became advocates for Manviya within the classroom. They not only ensured that she had access to safe food but also educated the rest of the class about the importance of respecting her condition. This collective effort helped create a more inclusive environment, where Manviya felt supported and understood, rather than isolated.

Each small step forward was a victory. As we continued to advocate for Manviya, we began to see the impact of our efforts. Her school was becoming a safer place, and she no longer felt like an outsider. Instead, she felt empowered and accepted, knowing that her peers and teachers understood her needs. This was one of the most significant milestones in our journey—the realization that education and awareness could transform an entire community.

? Spreading Awareness Among Friends and Family:

While we focused a lot of our efforts on restaurants and schools, one of the most crucial aspects of our advocacy was educating those closest to us—our friends and family. Despite their love for Manviya, many of them didn't fully understand the daily realities of living with celiac disease. To them, it seemed like an inconvenience rather than a life-threatening condition. They didn't realize that even a small crumb of gluten could have devastating consequences.

We started by having honest, open conversations with them. We explained how celiac disease wasn't just about avoiding gluten but about preventing it from entering Manviya's body in any form. Even shared utensils or cross-contact in the kitchen could trigger a reaction. To make it more tangible, we invited family and friends over and demonstrated how we prepared gluten-free meals. We showed them how careful we had to be to ensure that everything, from cutting boards to pans, was thoroughly cleaned.

These gatherings turned into learning experiences. Our loved ones asked questions, tried gluten-free recipes, and, most importantly, began to see the challenges we faced. Over time, they started to take more initiative in ensuring Manviya's safety. When we hosted gatherings, they would ask if a dish was safe for her to eat or take extra care when preparing meals. This shift in mindset was invaluable, and it made a huge difference in how we navigated our day-to-day lives.

By taking the time to educate those around us, we created a network of support that wasn't just passive but active. Our family and friends became part of the solution, contributing to Manviya's safety and well-being. They understood the importance of being vigilant, and their efforts helped foster a sense of community and empathy.

? The Importance of Cross-Contamination Prevention:

Throughout our advocacy journey, one of the most important lessons we learned was the significance of preventing cross-contamination. While avoiding gluten entirely is important, ensuring that no traces of gluten make their way into Manviya's food is equally essential. A small crumb, a shared utensil, or even an improperly cleaned surface could trigger a reaction that would be painful and potentially dangerous.

At home, we transformed our kitchen into a fortress against gluten. We invested in separate cutting boards, pans, toasters, and even dedicated cleaning supplies to ensure that every step of meal preparation was done with utmost care. We were meticulous in our approach—no shortcuts, no compromises. If anything touched gluten, it couldn't touch Manviya's food.

This vigilance didn't just apply at home. Whether we were dining at a restaurant or attending a social gathering, we had to be constant advocates for cross-contamination prevention. We explained to restaurant staff, teachers, and even friends how crucial it was to respect these boundaries. Over time, we saw that our efforts paid off. People became more mindful of the risks and started taking the necessary precautions. The simple act of ensuring that surfaces were properly cleaned or that utensils were dedicated to gluten-free foods made a significant difference.

Through this effort, we not only protected Manviya's health but also helped others understand the nuances of living with celiac disease. We learned that creating a gluten-free world isn't just about removing gluten from food—it's about preventing any risk, no matter how small.

? Celebrating Small Victories:

Our journey was long and often difficult, but we came to realize that it was the small victories that truly mattered. Whether it was a restaurant finally adopting proper cross-contamination protocols or a teacher taking the time to understand Manviya's needs, every success, no matter how small, reinforced the importance of our advocacy work.

Each small victory felt like a step forward—not just for Manviya but for every person living with celiac disease. It was a reminder that change, though slow, was happening. These moments kept us going, fuelled our determination, and reminded us why we were advocating in the first place.

? Building a Better Future:

Our advocacy efforts weren't just about managing our immediate challenges; they were about creating a world that would be safer for Manviya and others like her in the future. We wanted a world where celiac disease was understood, where restaurants, schools, and families took the necessary precautions, and where people living with the condition could thrive without fear of exposure.

With every conversation, every lesson learned, and every small victory, we were laying the foundation for that future. And though the journey was far from easy, it was clear that we were making a difference. Slowly, we were building a world where Manviya and others living with celiac disease would be respected, supported, and included in every space they entered. The road was long, but the impact of our advocacy was undeniable.

This journey, while challenging, became a testament to resilience, love, and hope. We knew that the work we were doing was bigger than just our family—it was part of a larger movement to create a more inclusive and understanding world. And with every victory, no matter how small, we were one step closer to achieving that goal.

CHAPTER NINE

EMBRACING THE JOURNEY – FUTURE AHEAD

Life with celiac disease is a unique journey, one that we walk as a family with love, growth, resilience, and unwavering determination. It has been a rollercoaster of emotions, but with every twist and turn, we've learned something new about each other and the strength we never knew we had. Through our princess's resilience, we've learned to confront challenges with courage and celebrate every small victory. Her journey is one of inspiration—teaching us that no obstacle is too insurmountable when faced together. As we look ahead, we see not just the unknown, but the power of hope, adaptation, and family.

? Reflecting on the Journey So Far:

As I watch Manviya smile, her face glowing with happiness as she enjoys one of her delicious gluten-free treats, a deep sense of gratitude fills my heart. Her happiness, a result of so much effort, is a testament to how far we've come. It hasn't always been easy. I remember the early days when we first discovered that she had celiac disease—days filled with uncertainty, confusion, and fear of the unknown. It felt like a fog had descended upon our lives, clouding our understanding and making each day seem like a series of daunting challenges.

At first, the world of gluten-free diets was foreign to us. Our kitchen, once brimming with an array of everyday foods, now became a battlefield of labels, research, and endless adjustments. The idea of navigating hospital visits, managing strict dietary restrictions, and dealing with daily changes in our routine seemed overwhelming. We had more questions than answers, and our hearts felt heavy with the thought of how this new reality might affect Manviya's future.

Yet, with each passing day, we found strength in each other. The weight of our worry never truly disappeared, but we learned to face it head-on. We learned that, despite the difficulties, we could still create a world full of joy, love, and belonging for our precious girl. The first months were filled with frustration, moments of tears as we watched Manviya struggle to understand why she couldn't join in birthday parties, why she felt isolated in social events, and why certain foods, once so familiar, became off-limits. The transition was painful, but as a family, we dug deep.

One of the biggest challenges was the emotional toll it took on her. Watching her grapple with feeling different, feeling left out, was heartbreaking. But with every trial, we found new ways to adapt, to innovate, and to make her feel included. We didn't just create new meals; we created new memories. We focused on the things she could do, rather than the things she couldn't. With patience and love, we became experts in reading food labels, advocating for her, and making sure she felt seen and valued—even when others didn't quite understand her needs.

Over time, we saw the fruits of our labour. Manviya's confidence grew, and so did our own understanding of this disease. Slowly but surely, we began to forge a new normal. We became part of a community of families who walked the same path, sharing stories, recipes, and advice. It wasn't long before we realized we weren't alone in this journey—there were other families, teachers, and even friends who rallied behind us, supporting us in ways that we hadn't imagined. We found strength in numbers.

Looking back, I realize just how much we've grown. What once seemed like insurmountable obstacles now feel like stepping stones. Every setback was an opportunity to learn, to grow, and to strengthen our bond as a family. We learned that the power of love and determination can conquer even the hardest challenges. More than managing the disease, we learned to live fully in spite of it.

? The Road Ahead:

While we have come so far, the road ahead still feels uncertain. Celiac disease is not something that can be "fixed" in the traditional sense. It is a lifelong journey that requires constant vigilance, adjustments, and a commitment to ensuring that Manviya's health and happiness remain a top priority. Yet, I've come to embrace this uncertainty. What once seemed daunting has now become a space for growth and opportunity. Though we can't predict every twist and turn ahead, we know one thing for certain: we will face them together, as a family.

We are ready for whatever comes next. With each new challenge, there is an opportunity for advocacy, education, and empowerment. We will continue to teach Manviya about her condition and how to navigate the world with confidence. As she grows older, there will be new situations—new social gatherings, new environments, and, undoubtedly, new hurdles. But I believe in her strength, and I believe in the power of the foundation we've built as a family. We have laid the groundwork for a future in which she can stand tall, never afraid to speak up for herself, and always equipped to face whatever challenges arise.

We've learned the importance of advocacy, not just for Manviya, but for everyone living with dietary restrictions. We will continue to push for awareness and acceptance—whether that means educating restaurants on gluten-free options, advocating for better support in schools, or simply offering a listening ear to another family facing similar struggles. It's a long road, but every effort we make, no matter how small, brings us one step closer to a more inclusive world.

The future may hold challenges that we can't yet foresee, but we have already built a network of support. Our family, friends, and the larger celiac community have become our lifeline, helping us through tough times and reminding us that we are never alone. These connections will continue to be our strength as we move forward into the future.

? Strengthening Resilience:

As we look to the future, one of our greatest priorities is to strengthen resilience—not just within ourselves, but in Manviya as well. Resilience has been the cornerstone of our journey, but we know that it's not enough to simply endure. Resilience is about thriving, about adapting to new circumstances, and about meeting life's challenges with grace and determination.

Manviya has been the living embodiment of resilience. I am constantly amazed by her ability to bounce back from setbacks, to embrace new challenges with curiosity and courage, and to maintain her joyful spirit despite the hurdles she faces. Her resilience is a beacon of strength for all of us, and we want to make sure she carries it with her throughout her life. We want her to know that she has everything she needs within herself to navigate any challenge, no matter how daunting it may seem.

It's easy to think of resilience as simply "getting through" tough times, but we've come to realize that resilience is about embracing change and growth. It's about looking at obstacles not as barriers, but as opportunities for learning and self-discovery. We want Manviya to internalize this mindset—that challenges are not roadblocks but stepping stones that shape her into the person she is meant to be. Her ability to see setbacks as chances for growth has already inspired us, and we are so proud of the resilient young woman she is becoming.

As we continue to foster resilience in her, we are preparing her for a future where she can face whatever life throws her way with confidence and poise. Celiac disease may be a part of her story, but it is not her story's defining feature. The resilience she's developed is the true foundation of her character, and it will carry her through every chapter of her life.

? Inspiring Change:

Our journey has also ignited a deep desire to inspire change—not just for Manviya, but for everyone who lives with dietary restrictions. We've witnessed the gaps in understanding and acceptance, and we've experienced firsthand the emotional toll of navigating a world that's not always accommodating. We've realized that change is needed, and we are committed to being part of that change.

Our advocacy isn't just about pushing for better resources or creating awareness; it's about shifting mindsets. It's about helping people understand that celiac disease is not just a "preference" or "lifestyle choice" but a serious medical condition that requires constant attention. It's about making spaces—whether schools, workplaces, or public events—more inclusive, ensuring that everyone, regardless of their dietary needs, can participate fully without fear of exclusion or harm.

As we continue to advocate for better awareness and understanding, we are not only supporting Manviya but also paving the way for others who face similar struggles. We hope that one day, children with any Gluten medical conditions will no longer feel like they are different or limited in their experiences. We envision a world where gluten-free options are readily available, and the emotional burden of explaining dietary needs is lessened.

Most importantly, we hope to empower Manviya to be a voice for change. She has already demonstrated such courage and resilience in her own journey, and we want to nurture that spirit. We want her to know that she has the power to not only navigate the world with celiac disease but to also be an advocate for others. As she grows older, we will continue to support her in finding her voice, knowing that she can be a catalyst for change, inspiring others to join the movement for a more inclusive and compassionate world.

? Looking Toward a Future of Empowerment:

Our dreams for the future are big, and they are filled with hope. We envision a world where celiac disease is no longer met with confusion or hesitation. Instead, it will be a world where gluten-free options are the norm, where schools, restaurants, and public spaces are fully equipped to accommodate those with dietary needs. We imagine a future where Manviya can walk into any restaurant and confidently order off the menu without worrying about cross-contamination.

This future isn't just about convenience or comfort. It's about empowerment. It's about giving Manviya the confidence to live her life fully, knowing that she is supported and that her needs will always be met. We want her to feel secure in her health and happiness, to never feel restricted by her condition, and to know that she is not alone in her journey.

Through our advocacy, we hope to create a ripple effect that spreads across society, changing attitudes and policies to ensure that people with celiac disease, and other dietary restrictions, can live their lives with dignity and respect. The world we envision is one where understanding and compassion are the foundation of every interaction, where no one has to feel isolated or unsafe because of their dietary needs.

? The Role of Family and Community:

Throughout this journey, the love and support of family and community have been our lifeline. As we look ahead, we know that this network of love and understanding will continue to play an essential role in Manviya's life. Our family has been our rock, and our friends and extended family have been an unwavering source of encouragement and strength. We know that we cannot do this alone.

The bonds we've formed with other families who share similar experiences have been invaluable. The celiac community has provided us with a sense of belonging, reminding us that we are never alone in this journey. These connections are not just about sharing tips or recipes—they are about building a support system that sustains us during difficult times and celebrates our victories with us.

In the years to come, we will continue to lean on these relationships, knowing that our community will always be there to offer guidance, support, and friendship. The strength of our family and the power of our community will be the pillars that support us as we continue this journey together.

? A Journey of Growth:

Looking back on this journey, it's clear that the challenges we've faced have not been in vain. They have shaped us, strengthened us, and taught us invaluable lessons. As a family, we have grown in ways we never could have imagined. We've learned to adapt, to support each other, and to embrace every challenge as an opportunity for growth.

Through Manviya's resilience, we have learned that growth is not always linear. It comes in waves, in small steps, and in moments of quiet strength. And every single moment has been worth it. We have become stronger, more compassionate, and more united than ever before. We've discovered beauty in the simple moments—whether it's sharing a meal, laughing together, or supporting each other through difficult times.

? Hope for the Future:

As we look to the future, our hearts are full of hope. The road ahead will undoubtedly be filled with challenges, but we believe that it will also be filled with opportunities for growth and change. With each step we take, we are moving closer to a world where celiac disease is understood, supported, and respected.

We know that the future holds endless possibilities for Manviya. We are committed to helping her chase her dreams, knowing that she is empowered, supported, and loved. The road ahead is unpredictable, but with love, resilience, and a community behind us, we will continue to walk this path with courage, optimism, and hope.

? The Final Lesson:

Reflecting on this journey, it becomes clear that the greatest lesson we've learned is that adversity does not define us. It is our response to adversity—our ability to rise above it—that shapes who we are. This journey has been a testament to the strength of our family, the power of love, and the importance of resilience. Through it all, we have learned that together, we can overcome anything.

In the face of difficulty, we have grown stronger, more connected, and more committed to spreading kindness and awareness. This journey has transformed us into a family that not only faces challenges with grace but embraces them with an unwavering belief in our collective ability to make a difference. And as we continue forward, we know that this journey is far from over—it's only just begun.

CHAPTER TEN

FEEDBACK

<u>Feedback forms</u>

This form is intended exclusively for individuals with medically diagnosed gluten-related conditions. If you do not have such a condition, we kindly request your assistance in sharing this form with others who may benefit from it. Your support will greatly contribute to our ongoing research efforts.

<u>https://forms.office.com/r/bPN6Ydj2e6</u>

Please scan it and fill the form

<u>For more information, please visit below links</u>

1. <u>https://www.blogger.com/blog/posts/322229861660685745S</u>
2. <u>https://www.facebook.com/profile.php?id=100093132319164</u>

List Of Additives And Preservatives Likely To Contain Gluten

Modified Starch (E1400–E1450)

Source: May be derived from wheat.

Examples:

E1400: Dextrin

E1410: Monostarch phosphate

E1420: Acetylated starch

E1450: Starch sodium octenyl succinate

Malt Extract and Malt Flavoring (No Code)

Source: Derived from barley.

Dextrin (E1400)

Source: May be wheat-based.

Caramel Color (E150a–E150d)

Source: Can be derived from barley malt.

Hydrolyzed Vegetable Protein (No Code)

Source: May be made from wheat.

Vegetable Gums (E410–E440)

Examples:

E414 (Acacia gum): May sometimes be processed with gluten-containing ingredients.

Emulsifiers (E471–E495)

Examples:

E471 (Mono- and diglycerides of fatty acids): May be processed with wheat.

Glucose Syrup (No Code)

Source: Can be derived from wheat.

Soy Sauce (No Code)

Source: Typically brewed with wheat.

Brewer's Yeast (No Code)

Source: A byproduct of beer brewing, potentially containing gluten from barley.

Seasonings and Spice Blends (No Code)

Source: May use wheat starch as a carrier.

Vegetable Proteins (No Code)

Source: Wheat gluten is sometimes used.

Thickening Agents (E1404)

Examples: Oxidized starch, which may be wheat-based.

Wheat-Based Thickeners (No Code)

Examples: Wheat starch is a common thickener.

Maltodextrin (No Code)

Source: May be derived from wheat or barley.

Artificial Sweeteners (E951)

Example: Aspartame, while typically gluten-free, can sometimes contain gluten-based carriers.

Natural Flavors (No Code)

Source: May occasionally be extracted using barley or wheat-based alcohol.

Stabilizers (E400–E495)

Examples:

E407 (Carrageenan): Rarely, but potentially processed with gluten.

.

.

.

.

Important Tips for Gluten-Free Living

These additives and preservatives can commonly be found in processed foods such as sauces, soups, snacks, baked goods, and seasonings. Always check ingredient labels, and when in doubt, contact manufacturers to confirm whether their products are gluten-free. If you have celiac disease or gluten intolerance, stick to certified gluten-free products for peace of mind.

Unexpected Places Gluten Might Be Hiding

Gluten can be found in surprising foods and products, even those that seem unlikely to contain wheat. Below are some common hidden sources:

1. Sauces and Condiments

Soy Sauce: Traditional soy sauce is made from wheat and barley. Use tamari for a gluten-free alternative.

Ketchup and Mustard: Certain brands may include malt vinegar or wheat-derived ingredients.

Dressings and Marinades: Processed options may contain hidden gluten. Opt for homemade or gluten-free labeled products.

2. Processed Meats

Sausages and Hot Dogs: Often contain wheat or barley-based fillers, breadcrumbs, or wheat gluten.

Deli Meats: Stabilizers or thickeners in some deli meats may include gluten.

3. Ice Cream

Some brands use wheat-based ingredients, such as cookie crumbs, malt, or gluten-containing stabilizers.

4. Candy

Licorice: Many brands use wheat flour as a binding agent.

Candy Coatings: Wheat flour may be used in coatings or as a thickener in some candies.

5. Alcoholic Beverages

Beer: Contains gluten unless specifically labeled gluten-free.

Whiskey: Distilled alcohols typically have minimal gluten, but individuals with severe sensitivity might still react.

6. Beverages

Coffee Creamers: Flavored or powdered creamers may contain gluten.

Flavored Teas: Pre-packaged teas with additives or flavorings might include barley or wheat.

7. Soups and Broths

Canned Soups: Often use gluten as a thickener or flavor enhancer. Choose gluten-free labeled or homemade soups.

8. Pharmaceuticals and Supplements

Pills and Medications: Some use gluten as a filler or binding agent.

Vitamins: Capsules or chewables may include gluten-based ingredients.

9. Oats

Non-Certified Oats: While naturally gluten-free, oats are often processed in facilities handling wheat, leading to cross-contamination. Choose certified gluten-free oats.

.

.

.

.

Important Tips

- Always read labels carefully. Gluten can be hidden under names like "malt," "modified starch," or "hydrolyzed protein."

- Be mindful of cross-contamination during manufacturing or preparation.

Epilogue: The Tapestry Of Love

As the final chapter closes, we find ourselves reflecting on the incredible journey of the Singh family—a story woven with threads of love, sacrifice, and resilience. Each character played a vital role in shaping their shared destiny.

Mr. Singh, a man of the world, found his greatest mission not on distant shores but in the warmth of his family. Mrs. Singh discovered a strength within herself that she never knew existed, balancing her dreams with the beautiful chaos of motherhood. And then there was Manviya, their beacon of light, whose courage and joy inspired them all, even as she faced her own challenges.

Parikshit, the little whirlwind of energy, reminded them every day that laughter and mischief are as essential to life as the air they breathe. Together, they created a life that was not without its trials but was always rich with love and meaning.

This story, however, is not just about one family—it is a celebration of everyone who has ever faced life's unexpected turns and emerged stronger. It is for those who find their strength in love and their joy in togetherness, even when life demands unexpected sacrifices.

As you turn the last page, may you carry with you the enduring lesson of the Singh family: that life's greatest treasures are not always found in the goals we chase, but in the love and connections we nurture along the way. Their story doesn't end here—it continues in every moment of laughter, in every tear of joy, and in the simple yet profound act of holding each other close.

May we all find joy beyond the challenges we face and strength in the love that surrounds us.